Day 1

GOD SAID YOU ARE *Strong*

_____
_____
_____
_____
_____
_____
_____
_____
_____
_____
_____
_____
_____
_____

> DRAW A PICTURE OR ICON THAT REPRESENTS YOUR STRENGTH

AFFIRMATION: *I am Strong*

GOD SAID YOU ARE *Loved*

ROMANS 5:8 SAYS...

"BUT GOD SHOWS HIS LOVE FOR US IN THAT WHILE WE WERE STILL SINNERS, CHRIST DIED FOR US." (ESV)

SIS...IT DOESN'T MATTER WHAT YOU'VE DONE GOD LOVES YOU ANYWAY....

I AFFIRM...TODAY I AM LOVED BECAUSE ....

_____
_____
_____
_____
_____
_____
_____
_____
_____
_____
_____
_____

AFFIRMATION: *I Am Loved*

Introduction

WELCOME TO YOUR 21 DAY GUIDE TO BECOMING A BETTER YOU, BY AFFIRMING THE THINGS YOU WISH TO MANIFEST IN YOUR LIFE. HERE @KNEWDESTINY WE WE RECOGNIZE THE STRUGGLE OF THE WORK-LIFE BALANCE. WE CREATED THIS JOURNAL FOR OUR OWN NEED OF SELF REFLECTION AND SELF CARE AND DECIDED WE NEEDED TO SHARE THIS WITH THE WORLD. WE BELIEVE IN WOMEN EMPOWERMENT AND SELF-LOVE! THEREFORE; WE ARE HERE TO TAKE THIS JOURNEY WITH YOU.

WE ARE BOTH BUSY MOMS, SISTERS, FRIENDS, CO-WORKERS, COUNSELORS, NURSES...GIRL THE LIST GOES ON. BUT..SELF-CARE IS IMPORTANT. HAVE YOU EVER HEARD THE SAYING, "YOU CAN'T POUR FROM AN EMPTY CUP". WELL IF YOU DON'T FEED YOUR SELF-CARE BUG AND FILL YOUR CUP, YOU WON'T BE ANY GOOD TO ANYONE IN YOUR LIFE.

WE WANT YOU TO AFFIRM TODAY THAT YOU WILL GO ON THIS JOURNEY WITH US. LET'S MANIFEST A HABIT OF POSITIVE AFFIRMATIONS IN YOUR LIFE. SIS... YOU KNOW IT TAKES 21 DAYS TO CREATE A HABIT AND 90 DAYS TO CREATE A LIFESTYLE. WELL... WE ARE ARE HERE TO HELP YOU GET STARTED.

REPEAT AFTER ME... I AFFIRM I HAVE THE WILLPOWER AND STRENGTH TO COMPLETE THIS 21 DAY JOURNEY BY AFFIRMING ALL POSITIVE THINGS IN MY LIFE EACH DAY. I AM COMMITTED TO CREATING A HEALTHY BALANCE IN MY LIFE. STEP ONE STARTS NOW.

KATHIA & DELISSA
KNEW DESTINY
FOLLOW US ON SOCIAL MEDIA

 @KNEWDESTINY

Day 1 _____

GOD SAID YOU ARE

PROVERBS 31:16-17 SAYS...

"SHE CONSIDERS A FIELD AND BUYS IT; WITH THE FRUIT OF HER HANDS SHE PLANTS A VINEYARD. SHE DRESSES HERSELF WITH STRENGTH AND MAKES HER ARMS STRONG." (ESV)

SIS...YOU CAN DO ANYTHING YOU PUT YOUR MIND TO. YOU CAN......

I AFFIRM....TODAY I AM STRONG BECAUSE...

_____
_____
_____
_____
_____
_____
_____
_____
_____
_____
_____
_____

AFFIRMATION: *I am Strong*

GOD SAID YOU ARE **Day 2** _____

Loved

_____
_____
_____
_____
_____
_____
_____
_____
_____
_____
_____
_____
_____

DRAW A PICTURE OR ICON THAT REPRESENTS YOUR LOVE

AFFIRMATION: *I Am Loved*

GOD SAID YOU ARE *Courageous*

JOSHUA 1:6 SAYS...

"BE STRONG AND COURAGEOUS, BECAUSE YOU WILL LEAD THESE PEOPLE TO INHERIT THE LAND I SWORE TO THEIR ANCESTORS TO GIVE THEM." (NIV)

SIS...BEING COURAGEOUS IS NOT AN ISOLATED TASK. YOUR COURAGE WILL CARRY ALONG IN YOUR LEGACY....

I AFFIRM..TODAY I AM COURAGEOUS BECAUSE...

_____
_____
_____
_____
_____
_____
_____
_____
_____
_____
_____
_____
_____
_____

AFFIRMATION: *I Am Courageous*

Day 3 _____

GOD SAID YOU ARE

Courageous

_____
_____
_____
_____
_____
_____
_____
_____
_____
_____
_____
_____

> DRAW A PICTURE OR ICON THAT REPRESENTS YOUR COURAGEOUSNESS

AFFIRMATION: *I Am Courageous*

Day 4

GOD SAID YOU ARE

PHILIPPIANS 4:6 SAYS...

"IN NOTHING BE ANXIOUS; BUT IN EVERYTHING BY PRAYER AND SUPPLICATION WITH THANKSGIVING LET YOUR REQUESTS BE MADE KNOWN UNTO GOD." (ASV)

SIS...YOU SPEAK AND GOD LISTENS. HE HEARS THE DESIRES OF YOUR HEART. TALK TO GOD, GIVE HIM YOUR REQUESTS. DO THE WORK AND BE PATIENT AND WAIT FOR HIM TO INTERCEDE ON YOUR BEHALF.

I AFFIRM..TODAY I AM PATIENT BECAUSE...

_____
_____
_____
_____
_____
_____
_____
_____
_____
_____
_____
_____

AFFIRMATION: *I Am Patient*

Day 4 _____

GOD SAID YOU ARE *Patient*

_____
_____
_____
_____
_____
_____
_____
_____
_____
_____
_____
_____
_____
_____

DRAW A PICTURE OR ICON THAT REPRESENTS YOUR PATIENCE

AFFIRMATION: *I Am Patient*

Day 5

GOD SAID YOU ARE
Confident

PSALM 27:3 SAYS...

"THOUGH AN ARMY BESIEGE ME, MY HEART WILL NOT FEAR THOUGH WAR BREAK OUT AGAINST ME, EVEN THEN I WILL BE CONFIDENT." (NIV)

SIS... YOU HAVE THE ABILITY TO SHOW CONFIDENCE IN EVERYTHING YOU DO. TRIALS AND TRIBULATIONS WILL ALWAYS COME..BUT.. YOU ARE QUEEN WHEN THE ENEMY COMES YOU HAVE THE SKILLS AND CONFIDENCE TO PUSH THROUGH....

AFFIRM...TODAY I AM CONFIDENT BECAUSE....

___

AFFIRMATION: *I Am Confident*

Day 5 _____

GOD SAID YOU ARE

Confident

_____
_____
_____
_____
_____
_____
_____
_____
_____
_____
_____
_____
_____

DRAW A PICTURE OR ICON THAT REPRESENTS YOUR CONFIDENCE

AFFIRMATION: *I Am Confident*

Day 6

GOD SAID YOU ARE *Dedicated*

I KINGS 8:61 SAYS...

"LET YOUR HEART THEREFORE BE WHOLLY DEVOTED TO THE LORD OUR GOD, TO WALK IN HIS STATUTES AND KEEP HIS COMMANDMENTS, AS THIS DAY" (ESV)

SIS...GOD KNOWS WHAT YOU ARE THINKING AND FEELING EVEN WHEN YOU FEEL ALONE. STAY DEDICATED TO KNOWING WHO AND WHOSE YOU ARE...

I AFFIRM...TODAY I AM DEDICATED BECAUSE...

_____
_____
_____
_____
_____
_____
_____
_____
_____
_____

AFFIRMATION: *I Am Dedicated*

GOD SAID YOU ARE **Day 6**

Dedicated

_____
_____
_____
_____
_____
_____
_____
_____
_____
_____
_____
_____

> DRAW A PICTURE OR ICON THAT REPRESENTS YOUR DEDICATION

AFFIRMATION: *I Am Dedicated*

GOD SAID YOU ARE

Day 7

ROMANS 8:24 SAYS...

"FOR WE ARE SAVED BY HOPE: BUT HOPE THAT IS SEEN IS NOT HOPE: FOR WHAT A MAN SEETH, WHY DOTH HE YET HOPE FOR?" (KJV)

SIS... HOPE IS PASSION FOR WHAT IS POSSIBLE...

I AFFIRM...I AM HOPEFUL BECAUSE...

_____
_____
_____
_____
_____
_____
_____
_____
_____
_____
_____
_____
_____
_____

AFFIRMATION: *I Am Hopeful*

Day 7

GOD SAID YOU ARE *Hopeful*

_____

DRAW A PICTURE OR ICON THAT REPRESENTS YOUR HOPEFULNESS

AFFIRMATION: *I Am Hopeful*

Reflection

SIS!! YOU MADE IT TO DAY 7. YOU ARE 1/3 OF THE WAY TO CREATING A HEALTHY AFFIRMING HABIT. LISTEN WE UNDERSTAND, IT WAS A STRUGGLE FOR US TOO. WE ARE IN THIS TOGETHER. WE ARE OUR SISTER'S KEEPER. KEEP PUSHING FORWARD. WE ARE ON OUR WAY TO A NEW LIFESTYLE BY AFFIRMING THE THINGS WE WANT TO MANIFEST IN OUR LIVES.

TAKE A MOMENT TO REFLECT ON YOUR JOURNEY THUS FAR. HOW ARE YOU FEELING? WHERE ARE YOU STILL STRUGGLING? GIVE YOURSELF A HIGH FIVE. YOU GOT THIS!!

_____
_____
_____
_____
_____
_____
_____
_____
_____
_____
_____
_____
_____
_____

Day 8

GOD SAID YOU ARE *Understanding*

PROVERBS 3:5-6 SAYS

"TRUST IN THE LORD WITH ALL THINE HEART; AND LEAN NOT UNTO THINE OWN UNDERSTANDING." (KJV)

SIS...UNDERSTANDING IS DEEPER THAN KNOWLEDGE. THERE ARE MANY PEOPLE WHO KNOW YOU, BUT THERE ARE VERY FEW WHOM UNDERSTAND YOU.

I AFFIRM...I AM UNDERSTANDING WITH MYSELF BECAUSE...

_____
_____
_____
_____
_____
_____
_____
_____
_____
_____
_____
_____
_____

AFFIRMATION: *I Am Understanding*

Day 8 _____

GOD SAID YOU ARE

Understanding

_____
_____
_____
_____
_____
_____
_____
_____
_____
_____
_____
_____
_____
_____

DRAW A PICTURE OR ICON THAT REPRESENTS YOUR UNDERSTANDING

AFFIRMATION: *I Am Understanding*

Day 9

GOD SAID YOU ARE

3 JOHN 1:2 SAYS...

"BELOVED, I WISH ABOVE ALL THINGS THAT THOU MAYEST PROSPER AND BE IN HEALTH, EVEN AS THY SOUL PROSPERETH." (KJV)

SIS...HARDWORK BRINGS PROSPERITY, PLAYING AROUND BRINGS POVERTY.

I AFFIRM...I AM PROSPEROUS BECAUSE...

_____
_____
_____
_____
_____
_____
_____
_____
_____
_____
_____
_____
_____

AFFIRMATION: *I Am Prosperous*

GOD SAID YOU ARE *Prosperous*

Day 9

DRAW A PICTURE OR ICON THAT REPRESENTS YOUR PROSPEROUSNESS

AFFIRMATION: *I Am Prosperous*

GOD SAID YOU ARE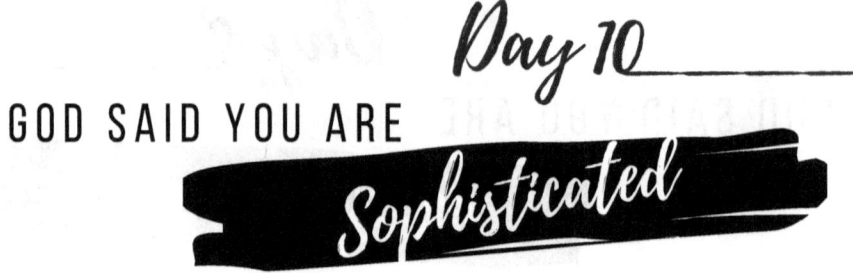

Day 10

LUKE 21:15 SAYS...

"FOR I WILL GIVE YOU WORDS AND WISDOM THAT NONE OF YOUR ADVERSARIES WILL BE ABLE TO RESIST OR CONTRADICT." (NIV)

SIS...EVOLVE RITUALS THAT SUPPORT A HIGHER LEVEL OF SELF WORTH

I AFFIRM...I AM SOPHISTICATED BECAUSE...

_____
_____
_____
_____
_____
_____
_____
_____
_____
_____
_____
_____
_____
_____
_____
_____

AFFIRMATION: *I Am Sophisticated*

Day 10

GOD SAID YOU ARE *Sophisticated*

_____
_____
_____
_____
_____
_____
_____
_____
_____
_____
_____
_____
_____

> DRAW A PICTURE OR ICON THAT REPRESENTS YOUR SOPHISTICATION

AFFIRMATION: *I Am Sophisticated*

Day 11

GOD SAID YOU ARE *A Leader*

"LUKE 6:31 SAYS...

"DO TO OTHERS AS YOU WOULD HAVE THEM DO TO YOU.." (NIV)

SIS...LEADERSHIP IS THE CAPACITY TO TRANSLATE VISION INTO REALITY. YOU ARE A LEADER...

I AFFIRM I AM A LEADER BECAUSE...

_____
_____
_____
_____
_____
_____
_____
_____
_____
_____
_____
_____

AFFIRMATION: *I Am A Leader*

Day 12

GOD SAID YOU ARE *A Leader*

DRAW A PICTURE OR ICON THAT REPRESENTS YOUR LEADERSHIP

AFFIRMATION: *I Am A Leader*

Day 12

GOD SAID YOU ARE

HEBREWS 4:16 SAYS...

"LET US THEN APPROACH GOD'S THRONE OF GRACE WITH CONFIDENCE, SO THAT WE MAY RECEIVE MERCY AND FIND GRACE TO HELP US IN OUR TIME OF NEED." (NIV)

SIS...HOLD YOURSELF TO A STANDARD OF GRACE, NOT PERFECTION.

I AFFIRM... I AM GRACEFUL BECAUSE...

_____
_____
_____
_____
_____
_____
_____
_____
_____
_____
_____
_____
_____
_____

AFFIRMATION: *I Am Graceful*

Day 12

GOD SAID YOU ARE *Graceful*

_____
_____
_____
_____
_____
_____
_____
_____
_____
_____
_____
_____

DRAW A PICTURE OR ICON THAT REPRESENTS YOUR GRACEFULNESS

AFFIRMATION: *I Am Graceful*

Day 13

GOD SAID YOU ARE

JAMES 4:10 SAYS...

"HUMBLE YOURSELVES BEFORE THE LORD AND HE WILL LIFT YOU UP" (NIV)

SIS...BEING HUMBLE IS KNOWING THAT YOU ARE NOT BETTER THAN ANYONE ELSE, BUT WISE ENOUGH TO KNOW THAT YOU ARE DIFFERENT.

I AFFIRM...I AM HUMBLE BECAUSE...

_____
_____
_____
_____
_____
_____
_____
_____
_____
_____
_____
_____

AFFIRMATION: *I Am Humble*

Day 13

GOD SAID YOU ARE *Humble*

DRAW A PICTURE OR ICON THAT REPRESENTS YOUR HUMBLENESS

AFFIRMATION: *I Am Humble*

Day 14

GOD SAID YOU ARE  Faithful

HEBREWS 11 SAYS...

"NOW FAITH IS THE SUBSTANCE OF THINGS HOPED FOR, THE EVIDENCE OF THINGS NOT SEEN." (KJV)

SIS...YOU MAY FEEL LIKE YOUR HARD WORK IS GOING UNNOTICED, STAY FAITHFUL TO THE PROCESS AND KNOW THAT GOD HAS YOUR BACK..

I AFFIRM...I AM FAITHFUL BECAUSE....

_____
_____
_____
_____
_____
_____
_____
_____
_____

AFFIRMATION: *I Am Faithful*

Day 14

GOD SAID YOU ARE

Faithufl

_____
_____
_____
_____
_____
_____
_____
_____
_____
_____
_____

DRAW A PICTURE OR ICON THAT REPRESENTS YOUR FAITHFULNESS

AFFIRMATION: *I Am Faithful*

SIS!! WE AT DAY 14..THATS 2/3 OF THE WAY TO CREATING A HEALTHY AFFIRMING HABIT. I DON'T KNOW IF THE WORLD IS GOING TO BE ABLE TO HANDLE THIS NEW YOU BOO!

TAKE A MOMENT TO REFLECT ON YOUR JOURNEY THIS FAR. HOW ARE YOU FEELING, WHERE ARE YOU STILL STRUGGLING, AND THEN GIVE YOURSELF A HIGH FIVE. YOU GOT THIS!!

_____
_____
_____
_____
_____
_____
_____
_____
_____
_____
_____
_____
_____
_____
_____

Day 15

GOD SAID YOU ARE

SONG OF SOLOMON 4:7 SAYS...

"YOU ARE ALTOGETHER BEAUTIFUL, MY DARLING, BEAUTIFUL IN EVERY WAY." (NIV)

SIS, IN CASE YOU DIDN'T KNOW, YOU ARE BEAUTIFUL!

I AFFIRM...I AM BEAUTIFUL INSIDE AND OUT BECAUSE.....

_____
_____
_____
_____
_____
_____
_____
_____
_____
_____
_____
_____
_____
_____

AFFIRMATION: *I Am Beautiful*

Day 15

GOD SAID YOU ARE *Beautiful*

_____
_____
_____
_____
_____
_____
_____
_____
_____
_____
_____

DRAW A PICTURE OR ICON THAT REPRESENTS YOUR BEAUTY

AFFIRMATION: *I Am Beautiful*

GOD SAID YOU ARE *Chosen* — Day 16

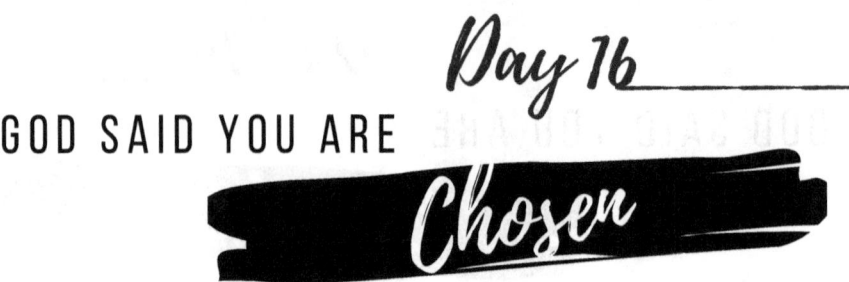

MATTHEW 22:14 SAYS...

"FOR MANY ARE INVITED, BUT FEW ARE CHOSEN." (NIV)

HONEY, WE CANT SPEAK FOR EVERYBODY BUT BABY GIRL YOU ARE CHOSEN!

I AFFIRM...I AM CHOSEN BECAUSE...

_____
_____
_____
_____
_____
_____
_____
_____
_____
_____
_____
_____
_____

AFFIRMATION: *I Am Chosen*

GOD SAID YOU ARE *Chosen*

Day 16

_____
_____
_____
_____
_____
_____
_____
_____
_____
_____
_____
_____
_____
_____
_____
_____

DRAW A PICTURE OR ICON THAT REPRESENTS YOU BEING CHOSEN

AFFIRMATION: *I Am Chosen*

Day 17

GOD SAID YOU ARE *Capable*

PHILIPPIANS 4:13 SAYS...

"I CAN DO ALL THINGS THROUGH CHRIST WHICH STRENGTHENETH ME.
." (KJV)

SIS...YOU ARE CAPABLE OF DOING WHATEVER IT IS IN LIFE THAT YOU WANT TO DO.

I AFFIRM...I AM CAPABLE OF.......BECAUSE.....

_____
_____
_____
_____
_____
_____
_____
_____
_____
_____
_____
_____
_____
_____

AFFIRMATION: *I Am Capable*

Day 17

GOD SAID YOU ARE

Capable

_____
_____
_____
_____
_____
_____
_____
_____
_____
_____
_____
_____
_____

DRAW A PICTURE OR ICON THAT REPRESENTS YOUR CAPABILITIES

AFFIRMATION: *I Am Capable*

GOD SAID YOU ARE *Enough*

Day 18

EPHESIANS 2:8 SAYS

"FOR IT IS BY GRACE YOU HAVE BEEN SAVED, THROUGH FAITH—AND THIS IS NOT FROM YOURSELVES, IT IS THE GIFT OF GOD" (NIV)

SIS...YOU ARE ENOUGH AND DON'T LET ANYONE TELL YOU DIFFERENT. JESUS LAID HIS LIFE DOWN FOR YOU. BABY, YOU ARE MORE THAN ENOUGH.

I AFFIRM...I AM MORE THAN ENOUGH BECAUSE...

_____
_____
_____
_____
_____
_____
_____
_____
_____
_____
_____
_____

AFFIRMATION: *I Am Enough*

GOD SAID YOU ARE *Enough* — Day 18

_____
_____
_____
_____
_____
_____
_____
_____
_____
_____
_____
_____
_____
_____

DRAW A PICTURE OR ICON THAT REPRESENTS WHY YOUR ARE ENOUGH

AFFIRMATION: *I Am Enough*

Day 19

GOD SAID YOU ARE

I CORINTHIANS 15:5 SAYS...

"BUT THANKS BE TO GOD! HE GIVES US THE VICTORY THROUGH OUR LORD JESUS CHRIST." (NIV)

SIS...YOU STEP OUT EVERYDAY KNOWING YOU HAVE THE VICTORY. KEEP YOUR HEAD UP HIGH AND LET'S CHANGE THE WORLD

I AFFIRM...I AM VICTORIOUS BECAUSE...

_____
_____
_____
_____
_____
_____
_____
_____
_____
_____

AFFIRMATION: *I Am Vicotorious*

GOD SAID YOU ARE *Victorious*

Day 19

_____
_____
_____
_____
_____
_____
_____
_____
_____
_____
_____
_____
_____

DRAW A PICTURE OR ICON THAT REPRESENTS YOUR VICTORY

AFFIRMATION: *I Am Vicotorious*

GOD SAID YOU ARE

Day 20

EPHESIANS 6:11 SAYS

"PUT ON THE FULL ARMOR OF GOD, SO THAT YOU WILL BE ABLE TO STAND FIRM AGAINST THE SCHEMES OF THE DEVIL." (NIV)

SIS...THE WORLD IS A COLD PLACE. YOU HAVE TO BE READY FOR WHATEVER THE DAY THROWS AT YOU. WE KNOW BEING A MOM WIFE, DAUGHTER, FRIEND, COUNSELOR, ETC TO EVERYONE CAN BE EXHAUSTING, BUT...GOD MADE YOU POWERFUL.

I AFFIRM...I AM POWERFUL BECAUSE...

_____
_____
_____
_____
_____
_____
_____
_____
_____
_____
_____

AFFIRMATION: *I Am Powerful*

Day 20

GOD SAID YOU ARE *Powerful*

_____
_____
_____
_____
_____
_____
_____
_____
_____
_____
_____
_____
_____

DRAW A PICTURE OR ICON THAT REPRESENTS YOUR POWER

AFFIRMATION: *I Am Powerful*

Day 21

GOD SAID YOU ARE *Conqueror*

JOB 42:2 SAYS...

"I KNOW THAT YOU CAN DO ALL THINGS; NO PURPOSE OF YOURS CAN BE THWARTED." (NIV)

SIS...YOU JUST CONQUERED 21 DAYS OF LOVING ON YOU, WHILE TAKING CARE OF THE HOUSE, KIDS, HUSBAND, COWORKERS, FRIENDS, AND THE DOG...BABY GIRL YOU ARE THE BOMB.COM. I WANT YOU TO SAY IT LOUD AND PROUD...

I AFFIRM I AM A CONQUEROR BECAUSE...

_____
_____
_____
_____
_____
_____
_____
_____
_____
_____

AFFIRMATION: *I Am A Conqueror*

Day 21

GOD SAID YOU ARE *Conqueror*

_____
_____
_____
_____
_____
_____
_____
_____
_____
_____
_____
_____
_____

DRAW A PICTURE OR ICON THAT REPRESENTS HOW YOU'VE CONQUERED

AFFIRMATION: *I Am A Conqueror*

Reflection

SIS..YOU CROSSED THE FINISH LINE. TAKE A BOW!! WE ARE SO PROUD OF YOU AND YOUR JOURNEY. YOU WERE COMMITTED, EVEN IF YOU FELL OFF, YOU MADE THE CHOICE TO PICK BACK UP AND FINISH THE RACE.

WE ARE SO BUSY AT TIMES, WE FORGET TO STOP AND CELEBRATE THE WINS. SIS... THIS WAS A HUGE ACCOMPLISHMENT. YOU SPENT THE PAST 21 DAYS CREATING A BETTER VERSION OF YOURSELF. WRITE TO GOD AND TELL HIM ABOUT YOUR JOURNEY.
GOD YOU SAID I COULD. I DID AND I FEEL...

_____
_____
_____
_____
_____
_____
_____
_____
_____
_____
_____
_____
_____
_____
_____
_____

Notes

Notes

Notes

Notes

Notes

Notes

Notes

www.ingramcontent.com/pod-product-compliance
Lightning Source LLC
Chambersburg PA
CBHW051703090426
42736CB00013B/2515